Lansdown Poets Anthology 2018

To Cline and Mandy

Best!

Tom

Lansdown Poets Anthology 2018

THE CHOIR PRESS

Copyright © 2018 Tony D'Arpino, Stephanie Codsi, David Punter,
Tim Burroughs, David Whitwell, Pete Milner, Joanna Butler,
Mark Sayers, Robin Kidson, Richard Devereux, David Cook,
R.C. Beavis, Gillie Harries, Pete Weinstock, Charles Thompson

All rights reserved. No part of this publication may be reproduced or
transmitted in any form or by any means, electronic or mechanical
including photocopying, recording or any information storage or
retrieval system, without prior permission in writing from the
publishers.

The rights of the individual poets to be identified as the authors of this
work have been asserted by them in accordance with the Copyright,
Designs and Patents Act 1988

First published in the United Kingdom in 2018 by
The Choir Press

ISBN 978-1-911589-34-1

Contents

Introduction	ix
Acknowledgements	xiv

Tony D'Arpino — 1

The Nova	2
Trading Holly	3
Wind	4
Clouds for Coleridge	5
The Levels	6

Stephanie Codsi — 8

Pluto's Two-Toned Heart	9
Cactus, Scorpion, Fire	10
To St Val	12
Song of Artemis	13
War by Occident	14

David Punter — 15

2017: Not Now	16
Night, Launderette, North Street	18
Love and Water	20
Dance Me	21
A Dream of Ships	22

Tim Burroughs   23

Cloud Study with John Constable   24
Imagine the Bees Stopped Buzzing   25
Shostakovich across the Trenches   26
Caravaggio – A Twisted Knife   28
If I Became a Stranger   36

David Whitwell   31

Deep in the Country   32
Sweet Red Apples   33
Come Away   34
Sweet Thames   35
Like The Sea   36

Pete Milner   37

Island   38
A Tonic for the Heart   42
Night Garden   44

Joanna Butler   45

Twisted History   46
Metamorphose   48
Switch   49
How She is Made   50
Tour   50

Mark Sayers 51

So Now Jane Has a Peke 52
Whilst I Have Tea in Bed Alone 53
A Eunuch Gently Playing a Lyre 54
Bringing to Mind Medea 56
Bringing That Awesome Reel to Heel 57

Robin Kidson 58

Canvey Island 59
These Bus Drivers 60
Being, Now, In Bywell 60
Magnolia Blossom 61
Pigeon English 62
The Viburnum Is Out 64

Richard Devereux 65

Embarking 66
For Alice 67
Bluebells 68
Oi Aprilianoi 69
Sonnet for Patrick Leigh Fermor 70
Ma 70

David Cook 71

Leaving Eden 72
A Last Look Before Leaving 73
The Past 74
Her Waking Truth 75
Lithograph 76
Acte Sans Paroles 77

R.C. Beavis	78
Limina	79
Pond	79
A Kite on Aldeburgh Beach	80
Albaicín	81
Pike O'Stickle	81
Nocturne	82
Little Venice	83
Excavation	84
Gillie Harries	85
Shelter	86
Gift	87
Everything Beautiful Has Edges	88
Eternal Creation	89
The Grace of Accuracy	90
Pete Weinstock	91
Under The Skin	92
Young Willows	94
A Bag of Dried Apricots	95
A Singularity	96
String Theory	97
Charles Thompson	98
Orpheus Laid Back in the Squat	99
I Remember You, a Hunting Girl	100
Now the Married Couple Dream	102
And So, Dear Friends, L'Avvocato	103
La Gioia	104

Introduction

In the wake of recent political shocks and their continuing repercussions, we need to reflect on identity. What makes us want to join, and what makes us want to separate, so as better to realise our selves and etch a trajectory towards a fruitful future? To separate is to individuate, the lyric moment; to join is the political moment, in all the many senses of that term – to move beyond while still working with the apparently ineluctable facts of gender, race, belief.

We need to celebrate the miracle of being alive; we need to resist the contentment that may come with privilege. Rilke said that 'the task of the poet is to praise'; generations of satirists have said that we need also to criticise – not in a dry, empty way but with a different act of celebration, of what we might imagine ourselves becoming if we could sweep away the dross. This is a collection: each voice is individual, but we would like to think they resound together, united in a hope, as Thomas Hardy said, that, despite – or because of – the difficulties, the doubts, 'it might be so'

David Cook / David Punter

Everywhere – with great excitement – one looks for the growth of soul. And I reflect on these 15 poets.

Tony D'Arpino is a surrealist whose startlingly off-kilter images present the reader a new world and appealingly so in succinct elliptical word-jazz rhythms. His poems have ground and this ground changes into something 'rich and strange', painterly, where the past and present fuse 'wrist sinuous drainage rhynes / droveways and scattered farms / the ancient wooden tracks / preserved by mother peat'. Here the old word 'droveways' brings the past alive into the poem with an American snap.

There is a sense of volcanic eruption in **Stephanie Codsi**, of surprising images which take in vast perspectives with great delight and energy and forge them in a new rendering. A beatnik kaleidoscope for now!

David Punter's *'Not Now'* is an angry lament for a deep British failure of sharing. Br ... I can't say the word. It is too hard and cold. 'Unite together / Don't make me laugh'. Underneath the anger there is a vision of compassion and a possibility of common healing experience, which in the now of the poem is achingly absent. It is a vision that illuminates *'Night, Launderette, North Street'* which deals with gentle ironic humour and kindness with the folk who wash their clothes 'in a well-ordered state'. These are poems of love, adventure, fable – a wide rich range underpinned by a core of feeling.

Tim Burroughs wears a coat of many colours. These are the colours of the painters he adores. They include Constable 'moulding them / as a new whole' and Caravaggio. Tim loves a good story and these stories make sense of complex events: 'German soldiers / said they knew they were beaten / when they heard / Shostakovitch across the trenches'. His eco-sense is affectionately and powerfully present with the bees on their 'wobbly dance'.

Pete Milner is a tale weaver so immersed in nature that his images are both symbolic and real in a way that I cannot separate. In *'Island'* 'a dark hat / floating in the shining water' is a mysterious image which makes the narrative surreal. In *'A Tonic to the Heart'* Pete sees nature and does something with it. He is a practical and poetic soul. *'Night Garden'* is Lawrentian.

In *'Twisted History'* **Joanna Butler** contrasts a cruel rich past with a cold timid present. The song of the past is more potent. 'This tune that seeps through fissures ... / Thunderous black birds'. She sings the joy of creating: 'Then the sculptor sings and hips / take shape'. She also sings the wild hard making of poetry 'up the steep ridge'. She describes the intensity of vision that is the gift of a passionate love.

∽ x ∾

I really like **David Whitwell's** meditative translucence. With what calm joy he throws off the yoke of philosophy. 'I can't remember the Philosophy / it's the orchard I recall.' I mark his poems as English Spiritual, 'a kind of solitude that is not inward-looking', independent, Blakean, searching for and finding a core of integral being and love in memory and childhood and gentle contact with the now. I am moved when I read his poem about his mother *'Like The Sea'*.

Mark Sayers is skillful with poetic form and, besides this, touching and funny. Courageously he is wry about himself. Solitude balances itself against resilient wit and insight. He makes me laugh.

Robin Kidson is as Northumbrian in his poetry as Basil Bunting. His voice is powerful and unique. He hymns Northumbria with skillful energy and affection 'These bus drivers, these working men, / Who fished for salmon in the Tyne'. There is an earthy music to his poems. The beat of his poetry is the beat of urgent life with motifs of survival, challenge, exhilaration.

Richard Devereux is a tender father in the three poems to his daughters. Any advice is bold, exuberant, alive: 'swing through the trees / flower in the desert / dance in the streets / stride, don't step'. Richard lives his own advice in his poems. He has a magnificent love affair with Greece and this finds learned and vital expression in his poetry.

David Cook is haunted by a bloodstained past: 'do we know in our bones / The violent history of our kind'. This different country of the past affirms the pagan. 'Distant crucifixion / Wild ... / luminous passion, more life'. He moves forward dynamically through the energies of the living. He charges his poems with acute insight into the subtle drama of significant moments.

R.C. Beavis is a poet of nature and of place. He has an excellent eye for light, movement and shape and how shapes converge upon each other. 'Grass, bank, strand shingled / Together, edging the world'. His writing – precise, elegant, lucid – ranges from the homeliness of Aldeburgh beach, where he flies a kite with his dad, to the exotic grandeur of Albaicín 'where ibn Negrala's ghost levitates peaceably above a Moorish / Chair'. As an archaeologist of knowledge and skill he is able to dramatize expertly the mixed emotions that attend an '*Excavation*': 'Trowelled up, a sacred confidence / has been broken'.

In '*Shelter*' **Gillie Harries** powerfully weaves a sensuous vision of the warm south. The poem brings together this vision with an erotic power and delicacy: 'the heave and push / Of mountain solidity / Grounds our tremble / With all this beauty'. In '*Gift*' Nature twines symbolically with the walkers in their passion which is both certain and uncertain. 'In front a river tips itself over limestone / Smoothed like the path we may choose'.

Pete Weinstock's poem '*Young Willows*' has an engaging, grounded vigour. 'We stumble through gorse / tripping, slipping, scrambled'. The poem fills itself with the exuberant language of a poet of piratical swagger. With earthy relish he celebrates the onion in '*Under The Skin*': 'You belong everywhere / revealing yourself coyly from the soil'. He plays wittily with Physics and Mathematics in '*A Singularity*' and '*String Theory*'.

Charles Thompson always relishes meeting those folk who are naturally jolly. Reading Chaucer is a great pleasure. Now he loves to remember some of the exuberant and wonderful people he met in Italy and word-paint them with as much accuracy and joy as he can muster. His deep interest in the feminine principle in mythologies informs many of his poems.

Many of the poets in this anthology have appeared at Poetry Can's Can Openers, The Berkeley Square Poetry Revue, and on BCFM.

These are the 15 poets in this anthology. I commend them to you. They speak with their hearts. Read them.

Charles Thompson

Diana Taylor works in film and photography. She worked for the BBC as a film editor, assistant producer and director. Whilst in London she was a freelance photographer. Her photographs were published in the Evening Standard, the Architects Journal, the English National Opera Review of the Year and the Museum of Mankind. Her work has been shown at the RWA and Bristol Salon.

Acknowledgements

I would like to thank Diana Taylor for the black-and-white photographs which so enhance the collection and Yvonne Devereux for her photograph of bluebells. I would also like to thank Amanda and Charles Yaxley, proprietors of the Lansdown Pub, Clifton Road, Clifton, and their staff for the use of the premises for our meetings, and for their hospitality.

Thank you also to the Choir Press for their expert help in the production of this volume.

There was a group of three editors. Many thanks, first, to David Cook whose very thorough and enthusiastic contribution to the project was a great help. Secondly, many thanks to David Punter for the erudite, professional and caring approach he brought to the project. As the third editor it has been an enormous pleasure working with everyone involved in this venture.

I would also like to thank Richard Devereux for generously offering many helpful suggestions as the anthology went forward.

Thank you too to all the poets who offered very good poetry with generosity and care. The editors are very grateful to them. **Charles Thompson**

Tony D'Arpino

Originally from Mount Holly, New Jersey, Tony D'Arpino has lived in California, Hawai'i, and Europe. Bristol has been his studio for a decade. '*Trading Holly*', '*Wind*', and '*The Levels*' were first published in *E Ratio* magazine, *The North* and *The Clearing* respectively. '*Clouds for Coleridge*' was commissioned for the map app Romantic Bristol: Writing the City, designed by the University of Bristol, Institute of Advanced Studies.

THE NOVA

The old joke,
I came to England by boat,
Disembarked here at this waterfront pub.
A day mark on courageous maps.
Avoiding the ephemera of Customs.

The old travel poster
Of a fisherman and a lighthouse,
Expose Yourself To Nova Scotia.
An atmosphere of ancient salt,
Seashells, cider, and songs.

My local is on an island
Of dancers, boat builders,
Poets and skippers
Still drinking the ghosts
Of the first next round.

An iceberg called alcohol,
A moon land fringed with the abyss
Of a back bar world of light
So bright with silver suns
The docks are our beer garden.

One lock for a floating harbour
And shining Cumberland Basin,
The waiting room in earlier times.
Many young lads drowned
And many pirates played the tides.

There's a boat built into the ceiling
Hung with oars, glass mugs, tackle
And gangways to an ancient chantry,
The folk club just upstairs,
Where whale songs, flamenco and jazz
Mix the music of five oceans.

TRADING HOLLY

'The girl in red is actually a sound'
                                        Roberto Bolaño

The ghost inside me
Feeds the marketplace
It's the mistletoe they want

A body of water
Suspended in mind
A primary pigment

Built into the old city walls
Was a bookshop
In winter code

A dealer in maps
Ephemerides of stars
And the blue sand of travel

A tiny plastic
Sun
Holding cloud cards

Commodity aesthetics
Of the holly thief
The market turns like fish

In pinwheel ice display
Singers and gamblers
Cakes and hats

I love holly
And the shadow
She casts

WIND

to Caroline

I can't find the hidden bridge
The August clouds of Rome
Illuminate a handwritten manuscript

I call you on the wind
Telephone towers
Sim card of simulacra

From the house of Cicero
Sorry closed
Come back tomorrow

In the Campo dei Fiori
A waitress swings an apron
If you don't drink I'm fired

And the secret society
Will burn the bronze statue
Of Giordano Bruno again so what

Scant minutes left
In the tower of wind
And the secret forests of Rome

I'm lost so I sleep
Patterns connect in paving stones
Concentric cobbles

Where fingers have traced a map
A body of stars and water
A dream bridge

I close my eyes and see you
At the tower on the bridge at Cahors
I call again and the wind says yes

CLOUDS FOR COLERIDGE

A clear invention
Of the imagination

A cloud looking
Like a phantom ship

With smoke and hair
Ghost involutes of sky

A tincture
Of cumulus humilis

At the edge of the gorge
Trees shaming the clouds

Coleridge
Watching the clouds

Coleridge isn't the poet
They wanted him to be

Outcast
Of the clouds

The poet invented
Islands for eyes

Too secular for the religious
Too religious for the secular

That cloud
Looks like an albatross

THE LEVELS

wrist sinuous drainage rhynes
droveways and scattered farms
the ancient wooden tracks
preserved by mother peat

jewelled jaws of the sea
settlements called huish
a family holding or 'worth'
enclosing oval infields

seahenge causeways
burrow wall beer wall
linked the islands
otters herons curlews

new rhynes and ditches
crack willows pollarded for hurdles
thatching spars
hay meadows

when the moon grew in the water
osier beds coppiced for wands
basketwork and fishtraps
alder beds and turbaries

the peat cut by hand
with the long-handled
square-bladed turf spade
the turves dried in cones and domes

the mouths of all the rivers
sealed by clyses
tidal sluices
closed against high tides

ley lines notched woodlands
ridge and furrow strip lynchets
the shape of terraced farms
lines in an open hand

Stephanie Codsi

A poet and singer song-writer, Steph has read and performed at Sanctum Bristol, BCfm, Falmouth university, and on the open-mic circuits in London and Bristol. Her poetry has been published on the map app: Romantic Bristol: Writing the City. Her poetry is often influenced by her song-writing. At times parodic and surreal, her writing is inspired by myth, metamorphosis, and strange landscapes.

She works as an Associate Lecturer of English and creative writing at the universities of Falmouth and Bristol, and has a PhD on the poetry of William Blake.

PLUTO'S TWO-TONED HEART

'We have now reached every planet in the solar system',
the last a triumph for the space probe to touch
Pluto's two-toned heart, that frozen ball of light
like a marble
   spinning in space
and cold as bone, an ice rock
tucked in the Kuiper Belt
                      orbiting
without pulse, its heart bleeding ice like a frozen lake
crusted over a dark
     body of water.

Pluto's two-toned heart, and its
five moons turning,
seem to emit sonic frequencies,
   sound waves of language inscrutable
transmitted into freakish blackness of space.

CACTUS, SCORPION, FIRE

(Cactus)
dry, dragon fire
rage
DRAGO-fly
grain of green
emerald seme

>rye contortion,
>cricket sun.
>buttress,
>fortress
>of emerald green, scree
>and dragon fire.
>crackled root
>cactus shoot
>hoot OWL and
>Viper-Sniper
>blackened crop.

(Scorpion)
scortched corp
pinched
shell blackened fortress
red earth
shiny in moon flight
flood blood
red earth and
clock rock scorpio
in moonlight

                                lick of tail fur
                  languid, langue, tongue of beast
                                tongue of heat.

                                         (Fire)
                                       heart beast:

                                         your lick
                                          of fire
                                 sings in seething –
                             flickering in fickle static

avowing   de-structing
                         I   reach out
                                         touching
                                                  you.

TO ST VAL

Darling saint, you give us our roses
of paper, our yearly obligations, mass
produced love-wishes, crosses and flowering
hearts of the nations.
This is no bitter reprimand, no portion of solitude.
Hangover of tradition with lack of vision: give me no
poses, no perfume, no rhyme stuck in thyme.
Instead why not
bring Venus and Cupid with you to the love parade,
freeing your care to the masses
with open arms.

SONG OF ARTEMIS

Patroness of wild things: wolvish, owl-dusk, bear and girl-child.
Heaving spear across the moon-flood moors.

Swift like arrow to anger, I shun the river-god, Alpheus,
and defeat the giants Aloadae with doe-fleeting deceit.

Deer and stag at my side, heart aperture wide as sky –
I can outrun any hunter; my quiver filled with arrowheads
cutting a narrow flight,

    like when Acteon spied to capture me, thieving a glance
at the pool on Mount Kithairon, game to ravage flesh to possess
the loveliness of my nymphs,
        I, bringer of death, brought down on him a spell,
and horns tore through his skull – four legs and a tail. So he fled –
his hounds pursued him, hungered for prey.

Once I knew a man. A giant in stature and attitude, and a match
for my hunting skills: he crowed he could kill at a
  hundred-mile distance.
Orion was his name,
and we hunted together until the gods – angered by
arrogance –
Stole him into death. His loved body
ornaments with lights the night sky.

I am Artemis,
undone with a kiss –

    my arrows shoot to great flight.

WAR BY OCCIDENT

War by occident an

error of judgement. Blinding

bombs scatter us into oblivion –

centripetal collapse, sucked cavity I'm

falling. Elemental universes shatter,

cleaving spirit from matter

another hatred is born

from a singular

mistake.

David Punter

David Punter has published five books of poetry with small presses, *China and Glass*, *Asleep at the Wheel*, *Lost in the Supermarket*, *Selected Short Stories* and *Foreign Ministry*, and has also published poems in a number of journals and magazines in the UK and overseas, including *PN Review* and *Encounter*. A lot of his earlier poems were essentially dreams; but he now finds himself writing, or trying to write, work with a more political edge. He performs with the poetry and music groups Echoes & Edges and Bearing Witness, and maintains a surreal blog at www.davidpunter.wordpress.com.

2017: NOT NOW

In response to Tony D'Arpino

Is this poem
skinny enough
for you? I used
to write in emerald
and gold
of hope in the dawn
evening glory.
Not now.

Spirits danced
in hedgerows
I was an occasional
victim of nostalgia
knife crime
and hatred of foreigners
were foreign to me.
Not now.

I wasn't naif;
I had a plan.
The State at the mercy
of capitalism
would implode,
and there would again
be a space for pleasure.
Not now.

Terror unleashed
on gays and blacks
makes me
(of course)
inarticulate.
Once I would have screamed
vivid pain.
Not now.

On through
the sad litany
of reversal,
rights lost,
centuries of labour
undone. Unite together?
Don't make me laugh.
Not now.

Outside my window
the harbour lights
blink red and green;
for one
to outdo the other
would spell calamity.
Do we care?
Not now.

I hoped
(and never really
knew I was hoping)
grass was green
and bosses were doomed
words could fill
the page.
Not now.

But you can't ignore
the rhythm building
if we all march in step
and keep to the line
we'll straighten out
this road to oblivion
and banish that skinny line.
Not now.

NIGHT, LAUNDERETTE, NORTH STREET

The washing-machine has broken down,
And so I am in a launderette.
It took me some time to find one.
There are launderettes in the student areas,
Of course, for when they do their own
Washing; but this is not that type of place.

It will close in ten minutes, I notice,
At 7.30. It has no practical reason
To close, it has no staff; but
It is very warm, like London's Circle Line,
And so if it stayed open people might
Come to huddle or sleep, or stare until dawn

At a circulation of socks; and that
Cannot be allowed, everybody in a well –
Ordered state must go home, must
Be housed before curfew. I am not sure
I am in a well-ordered state, my laundry
Is all over the place, I have the wrong coins.

Nor am I sure, as I peer out through
The steam, that everybody here in North Street
Is in a well-ordered state; the ragged T-shirt
And worn-out trainers of the guy
At the bus-stop outside suggest a person
Left cold, perhaps very cold, by boom and bust.

But in here it is warm, the shirts and knickers
revolve in interesting spirals. And from down the street,
as I look back, I see a promise of something
cosy, well-ordered; and so I give my useless
coins to a gruff, beseeching hand, of one
Not housed tonight; nor ordered; nor well-washed.

LOVE AND WATER

The clouds are piled like turrets formed of gold,
The silver water slides along the quay;
My morning body against your sleeping thigh,
The heron darts down from the moving tree.

Pale zebra-fish and green and purple wrasse
Trace rivulets of pattern on your arm
And incandescent colourings of delight
Break like defeated waves upon your calm.

Our love is like the water as it flows
Through channels to a landing-place unknown;
It imitates the starling as it glows
And brings forth all the glory in the bone.

DANCE ME

They sit at the Table of Mists, and they scowl
At the skulls and bright entrails that litter the ground.
Their hair's shocking colours illumine the sky –
Deep purples and emeralds from when they were drowned.

She says: 'Show me the man who's so fine in his heart
He can carry these milk-churns through rust and through flame
And I'll show him the light way through forest and heath
And he'll laugh when he finds he's forgotten his name'.

She says: 'Picture my bones as they grind and they lock,
All around the fair fields where the bald tigers roam,
And he'll call me his love and he'll call me his crown,
And exult when he finds that he's so far from home'.

She says: 'Write me the book of disgust and desire,
Where the liquids all flow and the song doesn't end;
My sisters and I have command of the air,
Twice dead, three times widowed; there's all time to mend'.

They bend to their knitting, they rise to their peak,
In delicate saffron, in flame and in lace,
They sing of the halo, they chant of the fire,
Their bodies are velvet, you cannot see their face,
Their words are of paper. There's nothing to trace.

A DREAM OF SHIPS

I dream of ships this colour-soaked spring morning,
Where bluebells wave in the green and the chaffinch trills,
The pale sea laps the ever-retreating sand-spit
Between the dry hedges of the hawthorned hills.

And all the ships are one ship, festooned with rigging,
A giant mermaid gaping at the prow,
The many windowed cabins gold and glowing,
The gangways ported for leaving, then as now.

And all the ships are different, galleons, dhows,
High-masted schooners, East India's joy and pride,
Merchantmen with polished decks all gleaming,
Cutters, and yawls, all waiting on the tide.

The captain stands right tall with arms akimbo,
Boom swing, halyards are tightened, great winds blow;
Outside the harbour lies the widow-maker,
Clothes dripping, weed-entangled, breathing slow.

But we must set out now upon these waters;
Bells clang, ropes shred, the hawsers rasp and strain.
There are lands to be explored, goods to bartered,
Metals for food, musket and ball for grain.

Salt-splattered, caulking sprung, unequal battles
With the violent ocean where all risks are great;
And slave-masters tell tales of death and triumph,
And every rescue comes too slow, too late.

So I dream of ships this dusk-enriched spring evening,
Where bats swerve as the colours fade away.
I dream, and down there in the Floating Harbour
Ghosts flit and whisper where the great ships lay.

Tim Burroughs

Tim, as a poet who also plays music and paints landscapes, likes to write about the fruitful fringes where poetry meets art, is surrounded by improvised music (especially sitar), where words come from the union of earth and sky, and their offspring is a shower of poetic phrases that fall, like leaves, to the ground.

His latest collection was "*Lament For Gaia-A Poet's Journey Through Eco Consciousness*". He has also been published in numerous anthologies. He performs regularly on the local poetry circuit, hosts SPEL, an alt poetry open mic, and co-hosts The Berkeley Square Poetry Revue with Charles Thompson. He is currently working on a collection of poems written in Cornwall.

CLOUD STUDY WITH JOHN CONSTABLE

that buff titanium bed
nestled in the corner
white wash
even over grainy paper
inrush of natural colour
dark side
darkened to Payne's grey
where the rain is forming
mixed with white
to let the light in
a primary blue lightened
with white
for that sky blue part
swirling splodgy wet brush
swirled like cotton wool
linking the parts
with mixes of base colours
moulding them
to form a whole
more buff at the base
with a lightness for clouds
then let the blue through
coeruleum
learnt from a master
a small part
of his majestic craft

IMAGINE THE BEES STOPPED BUZZING

Imagine the bees stopped buzzing
Silence amongst barren flowers
Hours without that tell-tale sign of summer.

These furry bright bringers of life
Wings whirring
Flitting between a thousand stamens
Flying laden with the sticky sugar of life
Taking food back to the hive
Mapping the route to the meadows
With a wobbly dance amongst
The jostling humming throng

Imagine silence in the wild flowers
No pollination of the fruit trees
A famine's emptiness echoing in the silent fields
The loss of the soft reassuring buzz
That constant dozy hum of summer

These busy barometers
Of the open field's health
Silenced by hive collapse
Hard workers brought down by mites
Poisoned by chemical sprays
Laid low by factory farming
These gentle bringers of fertility
Falling like still winged leaves
On the barren ground.

SHOSTAKOVICH ACROSS THE TRENCHES

a symphony
broadcast as a weapon
a statement of defiance
across snow swept trenches
starving musicians
stretching thin limbs
to build hope and resistance
to fascist tyranny

the repetition of marching drumbeats
become soaring horns and strings
of eventual Soviet victory
conductor's baton and composer's script
replacing jackboot and racist propaganda
flown back amidst medical supplies
finally played in St Petersburg
an elegy to the million who died
starving and shelled
a piece of bread a day
mummified corpses
wrapped and dragged to mass graves
dogs, cats and rats the only meat
a siege tan and hanging skin
so thin the bones showed

strengthened by great music
the citizens held out for three years
till the strings and trumpets heralded
the liberation by Soviet armies
the stranglehold of starvation released
captured German soldiers
said they knew they were beaten
when they heard
Shostakovich across the trenches

CARAVAGGIO – A TWISTED KNIFE

'ce genie enferme dans un taudis malsain'
(the genius confined in a filthy hole)
        Baudelaire, *Les Fleurs du Mal*

the knife or the crucifix
the dilemma of your life
the curse of your deaths
sharp razor edges
amongst rent boys
in period costume
ruffs and sneers
sawdust and jeers
the stiff joints of posing
washed away with chianti
as dark as blood
tempers spilled
in the hot course
of the chase
for love or lust
contour and shadow
silhouetted in the dusk
with muted service
always present
a jealous presence
watchful and always caring
up to your death in exile
hounded by baying magistrates
and corrupt bishops
for a crime of passion
always twisted
like the scar on your belly
the deadly kiss of your
blood brother

the knuckle fighter
with the sadist lip
who liked the crush of bone
as if smashed beneath his fist
or your groan as he entered you
you bailed him for a crime
he committed for you
to take out his rival
a woman in child
a bond stronger
than semen spilt
or the clasp of a bicep
the shadow of his alley blade
hovered over your head
like a gallows
as your spirit slipped to hell

IF I BECOME A STRANGER

If I become a stranger
my heart becomes too small
to have the space
to hold a soul
to hold anything at all

may my brain learn
some wisdom
may mind seek
some grace
may my hand
hold the hand
that is the human race
may my heart
burn with fire
know the truth of light
may the morning
banish forever
the darkness of the night

'cos my weakness
will remember
the shakiness within
when the possibilities
are endless
the things that lie within

diversity is knowledge
a learning of good things
a stretching of the limited
and the boundaries in between

David Whitwell

David Whitwell was born in the Wirral and grew up next to the River Dee. He studied medicine in London and philosophy in Oxford before following a career as a psychiatrist. He has lived in Bristol for many years, with Carolyn, his wife. He accompanied her many times to India when she was running a fair trade business. He is the author of *Recovery beyond Psychiatry* (2005) and his poem '*Barrow*' won the Lisa Thomas Poetry Prize for 2015. He has recently produced his first book of poems '*The Ruins of Summer*' (2017)

DEEP IN THE COUNTRY

Choosing time alone,
up in the hills
away from people,
as though all you want is yourself
and your own private world -
but it's not like that.

Those days under the trees,
feeling the wind,
waiting for rain,
create a heightened attentiveness.

As time passes
the mind moves outside itself
producing a kind of solitude
that is not inward looking.

Silence all around
leads to growing silence within.
Old arguments are replaced
by unexpected encounters.
Noises in the woods,
mist rising like smoke from the valley below.

Almost by accident
you learn to be free of thought.
You forget you are there,
a stone
lost in the wilderness.

SWEET RED APPLES

Yesterday I was trying to work,
but kept thinking of the orchard –
the one we had when I was a boy.
There was an old wooden shed
with a table and a chair,
and a window looking out at the trees.
One summer I sat there for days on end
reading philosophy
– while the apples ripened on the trees.
And it was good, even though
the reading was hard –
terrible dried up stuff.

The shed was old and dry
and gave off a wholesome woody smell.
The trees were weighed down
and the grass high
and blue with forget-me-nots.
And when my friends came they laughed
because I was reading Bertrand Russell.
We ate the sweet red apples
and went down to the shore
where we walked on the sand
and threw stones into the waves.
I can't remember the philosophy
or why I wanted to read it.
It's the orchard I recall
and going down to the beach
and feeling free
and having so much time.

COME AWAY

Think of all the wasted years,
piled up like …
out of date telephone directories –
full of people you no longer know.

Or maybe not.
Send them off to be recycled
so someone else can go through all the things
you no longer care to remember.

Come away, to an ale-house on the moors
with a log fire burning in the grate,
where we can sit all day
and talk of journeys we might have made
and the books we didn't write.

Don't think of things you leave behind
but keep on going
to places you never dreamed
would be on your itinerary.

Some breakthrough happened
while you were sleeping late
and now the world is different.
Things almost fantastical
are here within your reach.

SWEET THAMES

You'll find the steps going down
just below the Festival Hall.
And if you go there
when the tide is low,
you can walk upon the sand.
Children run and play,
and men with spades
look for things buried by the river.
Down there at the water's edge
the towers of the city rise up,
immense and magnificent,
while the stream, at your feet, flows on.
It's been like this since the Romans
built their fort on the north bank.

Here you feel the sun on your face,
hear the gulls and distant children.
It's beyond the reach of the law.
They are running wild, and
people of all ages are stripping off,
drinking, smoking,
lying about just as they please.

We are now below the city,
uncontaminated,
by all going on above.
Here the ancient river
still yields up its relics.
Artefacts, lost beyond recall,
brought back into the light.
A place to reconnect,
to rediscover firmer ground.

LIKE THE SEA

As we walked over flint and chalk,
high on the Salisbury Plain,
the wind ripped across fields of wheat,
waves breaking and twisting.

Look, she said, holding me close,
It's like the sea:
I could watch this for ever.

She came from the sea,
she was an *Island Girl*,
and loved it all her life.

Years later the farmer planted wheat
in the field behind our house,
and she caught it in a painting
- I have it still.
She is long gone,
and the house is no more.

This thing with the wheat,
for which there is no name,
I saw it again last summer,
on the cliffs at Mothecombe.
Again, in the sun and the wind,
I had to stand and watch.

Pete Milner

Peter Milner started writing poetry in his early thirties. He published a long narrative poem *'Taking Off'* in 1983. In several periods over the last thirty-odd years he's found himself writing for a living – explaining landscape in prose, usually in a succinct and highly disciplined manner. He may have finished with that work now but explorations of landscape and place remain important themes in much of his poetry.

ISLAND

From the café I saw,
over your shoulder
through the window
in the door,
an island out there
in the Channel –
a dark hat floating
in the shining water.

There's a cake
on a plate on the table
and behind your back
an island
framed like a small picture
of a dark hat
brimless in the brimming sea
rising from
the bright water.

I say,
'You can see the island.'
You turn and look
past the cranes and warehouses
in silhouette.
'Yes.'
'A dark hat,'
we agree.
We share the cake
drink the tea.

And afterwards we walk
along the terrace
slowly
towards the trees
wondering about the view
leaving behind a trail of words –
'… un-in-hab-it-ed' we say
except for birds …
and rats …
you've heard.
Swum out from somewhere …
'Must've done.'
Unless they came
before the waters rose
or something …
We carry on.

And in the Channel
clouds, with the shadows of clouds
are sailing over.

The light's paling
silvering and going grey.
Looks like a shower of rain
out there on its way –
drawing over a grey curtain.

So now we're thinking
about the inside of the car
parked
on the far side of the trees.
How far?

And the island,
if I can see it at all,
is a darker smudge
behind a veil of falling water
coming this way.

We talk. You say,
'We ought to walk
a little faster.'

And as we reach the trees
the first rain falls
pattering on the leaves,
as it has fallen on the island.
Then, as we reach the car
the hiss of rain upon the grass
'It's getting harder…'
And once we're inside
it runs in rivers down the glass.

'No point in going on 'til this is over
I suppose.'
I close my eyes or find
my eyes are closed
and behind my eyelids
a dim picture
like an illuminated sign
seen through a mist
of the island, dark
against a lit-up ocean.

The rain is roaring
on the roof.
I'm glad you're here,
glad you're with me.
Hold my hand.
I don't want to be alone now
and I wouldn't want to be
out there.

A TONIC FOR THE HEART

What a day it was
a high bright sunlit day
sky and sea
blue and luminescent.

In a grove of hawthorn trees
above the Channel –
the trees old
crabbed and looking so
but well-attired
and billowing with blossom.

We were
looking, looking ... looting
the white, pink inflorescence
because we were
filling up our carrier bags
with flowers
saying, 'sorry, thanks' and 'thank you'
to the trees repeatedly,
not just because
they looked
as if they might
fly into a rage
but because the flowers were beautiful
and smelt of something good –
we were making a decoction
then a tincture
(the flowers seeped in alcohol)
as a tonic for the heart.

Then with our bags of blossom
we walked the path along the clifftop –
a rush of green and
wind-shaped hedges
edged with yellow gorse
and bright pink campion
past beaches
caves and promontories
lost in colour.

We had to sit down
on the grass
and saw
twelve swans swimming on the sea
twelve swans white
the light melting
the blue ocean.

What a day it was –
that day it was
a tonic for the heart.

NIGHT GARDEN

At the edge
of autumn
first time
this side of summer
breath blows
visible
in the cooling air
my exhalation
mixing with shadow
and darkness welling
in the night garden
where
white flowers
ghost towers
tall
against a black hedge
stark
silent
clarions
sweet scented
deep throated
waiting for hawkmoths
that may not come.

While high above
my head
the moon wallows
in a cloudy bed.

Joanna Butler

Joanna is a poet, singer and piano player. Everything sparks the poetic, but influential moments include: her teacher banging out the rhythm to Blake's '*Holy Thursday*' on the school desks with the soles of his shoes; hearing Seamus Heaney talk about 'dreamtime' at Hay Festival 2006; touring as an actress in Spain and Ireland; and, in 2016, meeting Patti Smith by chance in Paris, next to a sign tied to some church railings that read, '*The World is Poetry*'. Joanna has given readings at Bristol Central Library, Bristol Folk Festival, Tate Modern, The National Gallery and The Poetry Café.

TWISTED HISTORY

An ashtray stuffed with stubs
at the archaeologist's office in Aguilar
del Rio Alhama.
Things have been fraught.

*At the swimming pool earlier,
a vulture circled overhead.*

Shelf upon shelf of buff boxes.
Remains numbered. All numbered.

*I am told to make puppets.
So I twist my wires, cannot
get the vulture out of my head.*

We pass round artefacts,
cradling orange pots like children
fearful of dropping the past.

A Celt-Iberian horse-bell sounds
erasing the songs of myself,
my shoulders, my arms,
my hands that shape each wire.

*This tune that seeps through fissures,
vulture spirits crossing boundaries
of blood and skin
into my country.*

Thunderous black birds
circling and surrounding.
Wings beating.

*Romans brought a party of flame,
set this place alight.*

Wings beating.

I touch the burnt stone of the city wall,
the shivers that rent the ground.
My palms are scorch-marked by time.

I am told to make puppets.
I pull a dry bone from the stone.

METAMORPHOSE

Something pulled a wing
off my back.

I looked at the workers.
Not one of them.

Something in the invisible
secreted this in my breast

where it grew ascetic
pacing its skeletal cell.

A sensation of falling
cocooned my heart.

Something kept rearing
in my voice box:

a hardy winter hind revelling
in a new sharp cold

blossom of spring.

SWITCH

I lay in bed.
Whispered your name to the air.

You were not beside me
because of
oh
complications
constraints.

Our situation.

As the whisper finished,
my lips folding
into a smile,
I saw through the lace curtain
the afternoon's low sun
raise the level of its brilliance
fire up the green of the fir.
Heard the wingbeat announcing arrival.
Homing pigeons flying their circular flock.

As if the whisper through my lips
had flicked a switch.

HOW SHE IS MADE

She does not come together all at once
but slowly over time, and piece by piece.
Not knowing is where it begins, the dunce
cap is worn by artists first to release
simple decisions that must come before
the clay dries.
                Then the sculptor sings and hips
take shape, feet stride out from under the raw
folds of the dress that curve up to the lips.
Still but half-made, there is so much movement
in her emerging that I hear new song
pierce the measured ticking of the day, bent
on reaching those who've known silence too long.
From handfuls of clay the sculptor prises
out the lost world where a woman rises.

TOUR

We walked on the beach and smelt the sun rise
its glare harsh-white over the West Coast rock.
Tired from the tour, too-early starts, days spent
cramped in a van, journeys over pot-holes,
we watched Atlantic waves crash into shore.

Tired from playing the same words over
and over, missing places we recognised.
A school stood by the dunes, a bare playground,
a wall plaque to remember a pupil
who had died aged nine.

                              All these things gathered.

Late in the day, time turned into sounds:
straining metal like an old iron boat
desperate to reach the horizon before night.
The tour-bus falling, locked in a current,
spinning the final slam against the wall.

Mark Sayers

Mark Sayers lives on his own and writing poetry and attending poetry groups keeps him sane!

SO NOW JANE HAS A PEKE

Why do some ladies find that men
Are something they can do without?
'They're thoughtless, selfish, beyond doubt,
And have a tendency to snore.'
So women dream and have a yen
To show *that man* the open door.

So what if men claim they adore
To be with her? 'For all that means
Is that *Jane slaves* or there'll be scenes
And temper tantrums if I fail
To cook enough when Matt begs, "More?".
Then when I say, "No!", he will rail!'

Sadly, we can't forget the tales
Of Barmaid Jade and Matt's *faux pas*
Or when he, fresh from The Star's bar,
Comes staggering home and then insists
On seeing Jane's birthday suit, bewails
When she says, 'I'm tired', and desists.

Jane looks back, 'Bet Matt will persist
In thinking that all love his verse
At dinner, whilst guests squirm and purse
Their lips as he bores them to bits,
Some ladies finding him sexist.' ...
It's no surprise to learn she quits.

So now Jane has a Peke who sits
By the fire or lolls on her lap,
With silken hair and no cloth cap;
Who loves her each and every day
And doesn't pique her, as befits. ...
She sees John sometimes, who is gay.

WHILST I HAVE TEA IN BED ALONE

Why can't some woman telephone?
Only my sister now rings me
Whilst I have tea in bed alone.

Who says I mustn't have a moan?
I want a widow, divorcee!
Why can't some woman telephone?

No crone or thick-skinned snooty Sloane;
No neurosis, kindness the key, ...
Whilst I have tea in bed, alone.

Someone who's cuddly and is prone
To smooching, snug on my settee.
Why can't some woman telephone?

So feminine, she'll have no bone
To pick with me, and such *esprit*, ...
Whilst I have tea in bed, ... alone!

I miss that droning, phoning tone,
'Good Lady, did you hear my plea?'.
Why can't some woman telephone
Whilst I have tea in bed alone?

A EUNUCH GENTLY PLAYING THE LYRE

She's black and beautiful, austere,
And perched up in her corner seat.
Long hair in ringlets, ... quite offbeat.
Has she stepped off a movie set?
I find it so hard not to peer.
Is this pensive nymphet upset?

A hint of inky bosom winks,
Her eyes are like two coals of fire.
A desert storm fans my desire
To feel those emerald fingernails
Coax me. A kiss, before she sinks
And slowly lets down all her sails. ...

She's lazing now in her boudoir
With slaves alert in case she calls;
Her voice echoes down marble halls
In Tunis, Tobago or Tyre.
Songs from a soothing, dusky choir,
A eunuch gently playing the lyre.

What lures her on the X39
To Bath and where's her camel train?
She must find us all so mundane,
What on earth tempts her to the Styx?
How could I make this maiden mine,
To please and pamper this phoenix?

Why not a house on Sion Hill
Where she could gaze at Brunel's Bridge,
Sip Champagne, ice-cold from the fridge,
Whilst lazing on the balcony,
My arm round her to stop a chill?
Is the lady called Harmony?

She leaves the bus in Albion Place,
We turn down Little Stanhope Street;
Bath seems so quaint, out of the heat:
No swaying dancers, beating drums,
But Georgian splendour keeping pace
With challenges ... and girls' bare tums.

BRINGING TO MIND MEDEA

I do so admire clever folk
Who can write poems that sound like prose.
Anything goes, so some suppose
Unusual words must be a cloak
For something brilliant to provoke
Earnest discussion on those rows
With dialect and such *bon mots*
'To quote Homer's a master-stroke!'

But first ensure therè's nothing clear,
Impugning and doubt are a boon.
'What could he mean? It's so obscure
And somehow brings to mind Medea.
I can't wait. His next book's out soon
With phrases which have such allure!'

BRINGING THAT AWESOME REEL TO HEEL

Her look of scorn still bores through me
Stumbling through **The Lammermuir Hills**,
Paying **Tribute to the Borders** fills
Me with dread, for I'll not construe
How I can toss that tartan tree
To make the Scottish Dance breakthrough.

The **Moray Rant** is a nightmare:
Dancing between the 2s and 3s.
Designed, so I feel ill at ease.
God knows how any master this!
It's no good, for I cannot bear
To hear her hiss from the abyss.

The ladies flee at my approach
In case they hear those dreaded words.
They'd sooner dance with Kurds, jailbirds
Than me, so I'm left on my own.
If I was rich, a comely Coach
Would somehow give me some backbone

And show me what I have to do.
It's no good giving me a list
Which I forget. She must assist
With 'Who's my corner? What Half Reel?'
To help lasso and so subdue
And bring that awesome Reel to heel.

Beginners' Dance? There's not a chance
That I will grace that august Hall
Where everybody has a ball,
Except me, feeling like a prune!
In The Grapes none set nor advance
So, from those glances I'm immune.

Robin Kidson

Robin Kidson was born and bred in a remote part of rural Northumberland but now lives near Bristol. He has a compulsion to write poems on a range of subjects including the North, class, birds and music.

CANVEY ISLAND

Lee Brilleaux 1952–1994

Low-lying land looked down upon,
By big skies and a snarling city.
Muddy waters creeping through,
Tarry creeks and oily marshes.
Howling wolves across the sea,
Calling you to New Orleans,
Mississippi, Tennessee ...

Good Canvey Island boys say their prayers,
In the voices of Essex and London,
But they sing in American.
Gulls cry in estuarine falsetto;
Girls cry ... tears and oil flow,
Lubricating old England,
So she goes so free and easy.

Somewhere, there's the smell
Of sweat and stale beer,
And the sound of a bass beat
Stamping on your ears.
Spew, piss, Brut, cheap shampoo,
The stink of electricity,
A boy singing the blues.

They live level with the sea
On Canvey Island,
Oil and salty water on their lips.
To a soundtrack of *Smokestack Lightning*,
They dream of the next storm, the next high tide,
The ride on the crest of the tsunami wave;
If you don't wake up, you drown.

Doctor Feelgood will see you now.
He'll give you stuff, to bring you up
To higher, drier ground.

THESE BUS DRIVERS

Ray made his own smoker.
Him and Dad used it to smoke salmon
They'd caught in the cold brown Tyne.
'We live like kings', they said,
These bus drivers, these working men,
Who fished for salmon in the Tyne,
And shot wild duck by the Erring Burn,
And ruled the universe.

BEING, NOW, IN BYWELL
For Piper

I want to show my southron granddaughter
The family graves at Bywell;
I want her to know
That she's part of a straight and steady line.
I want her to hear the trickle of the Tyne,
The music that accompanies
All these journeys to eternity.
I want her to see the spot,
Where Bunting and Ginsberg stood
By Bywell Cross.
I want her to hear
The stories that were told to me.
But all she wants to do
Is run round and round the church,
Thread a loose and loopy line
In and out of the grassy graves;
And, in the end, I give in;
The dead and the past have their place,
But not today;
Today is for the joy of living,
For the young and the new,
For the birds singing,
For the laughter of a little girl,
For being, now, in Bywell.

MAGNOLIA BLOSSOM

Magnolia blossom doesn't last long;
Already, it's dripping down to the ground;
The petals like pink-edged flakes of white fish,
Haddock and cod, whiting and hake.

A feminine hand grips the steering wheel
So hard, the knuckles are angry and white.
She wears sunglasses, though there is no sun.
The car over-revs away, squealing
In a rage of black rubber and dust,
Crushing the magnolia blossom
Which, in any case, is already turning
From pristine white to grey, brown, sticky black,
And insinuating itself
Into the tarmac.

She does not know the names of things,
Nor the history of her land,
Nor the reasons why magnolias blossom,
Birds fly, and fish swim in the sea;
But she knows her worth, and that she is
Desirable. She will come to a sticky end.

Magnolia blossom doesn't last long;
Already, it's fading into the ground;
The petals like flakes of rotting white fish,
Haddock and cod, whiting and hake.

PIGEON ENGLISH

Uncle Jack (my dad's cousin) kept pigeons,
Which compelled him to speak in a foreign tongue:
Pigeon English, for want of a better term,
Cree, skem, Up North Combine, cushat, kellick, chirm.

Uncle Jack, on Saturday afternoons,
Waiting for his children to come home,
From far away towns in the south country,
Or further afield: Flanders, Normandy.

Uncle Jack, on Saturday afternoons,
With wireless tuned to the football results:
'Newcastle United, nil ...' oh, ye bugger;
Haway, me bloody skemmies, come on hyem.

And then the familiar cooing croon,
As his pigeons return one by one,
And the mystery's good for another afternoon,
Fligged, ducket, stobbie, flacker, squeaker, glead.

Uncle Jack on summer Sunday mornings;
Two-Way Family Favourites on the airwaves,
Johnny Mathis, Nat King Cole, Doris Day;
The smell of roasting beef and rotting cabbage.

Uncle Jack on summer Sunday mornings,
Letting his pigeons run free in the sky.
They twirl and turn like shoals of herring,
Spitfire squadrons, Lancaster bombers.

The skems feel like extensions of his arms;
He is up there, feathered, flying with them;
On summer Sunday mornings, he owns the skies
Of Stocksfield, Mickley, Bywell, Branch End.

He told me once that the Queen kept pigeons.
I imagined her in a rose headscarf,
Handling pigeons in a makeshift cree,
In the gardens of Buckingham Palace.

In later years, when the times got vulgar,
He developed a drag act for the clubs.
I don't know what happened to the pigeons,
The *cushats, stobbies, squeakers, kellicks, skems.*

THE VIBURNUM IS OUT

The viburnum is out, smelling of girls.
Today, the whole world smells of viburnum.
Amazon armies invade my garden,
Crushing the daffodil resistance.

The viburnum is out, smelling of fox.
A fox city has been built underground,
With fox pharmacies, fox brothels, fox banks.
Bureaucrats at their Ministry of War
Are preparing a pre-emptive attack.
The Thought-Foxes are having a re-think,
About camouflaging their short, sharp stink.

The viburnum is out, smelling of ...
Something else wild. Badger pelt? Deer hide?
The tightly packed feathers of a merlin?
An old wildness has reclaimed the garden.
Adam and Eve have packed their bags and left;
The serpent has lost its voice and shed its skin,
And become a gentle slowworm again.
Innocence is back, a state of grace pertains.

Emboldened by the new dispensations,
Buzzards flutter awkwardly down from their sky,
And give the slowworm a slow and savage
Requiem. There's no sin now in Eden.

Richard Devereux

Richard Devereux dipped his toes back in the poetry world four years ago after falling silent for some thirty years. He considers he was fortunate to land among the Lansdown Poets. He feels part of a long tradition of poets meeting to share their work and receive encouragement and inspiration from their fellows.

Richard has recently published his first collection, *Bill*, which tells the story of his grandfather, a soldier of the First World War who fought in Greece. He represents Private Everyman. The poem '*Ma*' is about Bill's mother. Three other poems are about his own daughters. Richard lived and taught English in Athens. Greece informs and influences much of his writing.

EMBARKING

for Sarah as she goes travelling

Sometimes a leaving
is much more than departing.
Such a setting off
and leaving behind
has to be called 'embarking'.

With a single step,
at a singular moment,
the most momentous journey starts
when one foot lifts,
swings forward,

grounds to complete the step.
Flex the soles of your feet
and assume the moment.
Take one look back
at your hinterland

then be blown on the breeze
swing through the trees
flower in the desert
dance in the streets
stride, don't step,

absorb everything,
regret nothing.
Then slow, and listen
to an old woman and a boy
and to the humming of the moon.

FOR ALICE

on her Eighteenth Birthday

The most momentous day of all is come –
the vernal equinox when earth attains
a true alignment with the sun, then on
she'll tilt and spin as she has ever done.

To sound of pipes above an ancient site,
a bud of light at dawn becomes a bloom.
New energies are soon to be released
when birds adorn the break of day with song.

But Alice is asleep and does not stir;
she was a child, but is a child no more.
As yet she's unaware the day has come
when she must shed the chrysalis of youth.

It's time for her to spread her wings and fly.
Some butterflies delight and flutter by,
alighting on the hollyhock and sage,
while others seem to fly with more intent.

May Alice be admired by those who see
in her a grace and beauty unawares.
May she be treated well by those she loves:
my hopes for her today – now she's eighteen.

BLUEBELLS

bluebells and beyond the bluebells bluebells
a whole hill-side of bluebells
the famous Blackhill bluebells
May Day bluebells
run-away bluebells
scampering bluebells
drawn to the sunshine – sunshine bluebells
ding-a-ling bluebells
my little girl lies in the bluebells
in the long grasses and bluebells
her hair is dressed with bluebells
I see a painting – girl in the bluebells
a cry of pain – from the bluebells
my girl is hurt – stung – forget the bloody bluebells
she's been stung by a bee in the bluebells
no – by a stinging nettle nestling in the bluebells
there is always a nettle
in the bluebells

OI APRILIANOI

The Aprils
A great name for a band –
lyre, pipes and mandolin.
Or a folk-dance troupe.
Or a gangster film.

Oi Aprilianoi – The Colonels:
that ring of sad and vicious clowns
who staged the April Coup [1].
The graduates of Hero School
were tyro-tyrants, middle-rankers

men with lists: targets to be taken
from their beds at the prod of a gun;
locations to secure –
tanks parked up outside;
playlists for the radio station.

One took along his case of 78's
so all could spin and wheel
to upright military marches,
in between A Voice repeating
We Are in Charge, We Give the Orders.

It was a text-book Coup.
Democracy squealed, squeaked
and was silent.

---

[1] on 21 April 1967 in Athens

SONNET FOR PATRICK LEIGH FERMOR

Expelled, though Paddy claimed he only talked
To the girl. Now left to teach himself, he read
Till words became the cords that strung his soul.
And when Bohemian London palled, he walked,
In ditches and in castles laid his head,
From The Hook, 'cross restless Europe to his goal:
Constantinople. Low or high the roads
He took and, ever in his hand, *The Odes.*

The dashing figure, sword in hand, on horse,
Soon left The Blues. A maverick, of course,
Is best set free and left to soar and swoop.
Now Paddy's band pulled off their daring *coup*
And snatched the German General Kreipe! Crete,
With lyres and *mantinadas,* marks their feat.

MA

was strong
she carried crosses
bore burdens

lived by the strength
of her own arms
in the laundry

and by the bread
left in the porch of the church
for widows

David Cook

I retired from Psychiatry three years ago, and look back now to a younger centre of consciousness with complex feelings. I am not an empiricist and have no hesitation in describing that centre as me, my younger self. I remember being much exercised by relationship and career uncertainties which have long since ceased to be part of my life. I suppose back then I resolved problems through my own efforts, or with the help of friends, or else they moved beyond my influence or interest. Have these difficulties marked me, as timber is marked by a knot at a dividing of the ways? Or is that too physical a simile to capture what is important in a human history, scarring and healing being not quite the same? Is there something creative in overcoming difficulty which works itself into the future of the agent? Sometimes, as when under duress, I sense even now an energy pent up from those old struggles. In dreams, whole fictions, involving friends and loved ones and spun it would seem from chaos, assemble as if to remind me of how past intimacies are never finally rendered. The fragility of hope, its too brief visitations, the crush of its extinction: these bring their own atmosphere to the homeward journey. And yes, always, the renewal of hope; the inspiration of those one loves and admires. Touch wood.

And so poetry, like our lives: multifarious. Poetry, unlike our lives: shapely, economical, lucid.

LEAVING EDEN

No whence or whither in this early memory,
just its bright singular presence.
Why has it stayed with me?
Is it a clue to what dragged me into thought?
If feeling and thinking are held there in one kernel
can I prise them apart?
It must date from a time
when noises and single words did the work of sentences,
accompanied now and then by flailing arms.
Luckily mother was there to respond and give meaning,
but from the memory itself she is absent.

I sit beneath a round table, a cloth falling over its edge.
Sunlight reaches me through a window looking onto lawn.
In front of me a woman is seated,
head and shoulders hidden by the table's surface.
There is a heavy, familiar scent.
Her dress is pulled up revealing a suspender and grey stocking
and above it parchment coloured skin.
I look closely.
The expanse is covered with delicate wrinkles.
She pushes the needle of a syringe into her skin,
and as she does so
a bead of crimson blood appears.
It holds its shape for ever.
The memory ends without a word being spoken or sound made.

I can split the memory in two,
into curiosity and bewilderment.
The curiosity could be expressed as
"What is happening here?"
the bewilderment as

"Am I supposed to be seeing this?"
which further resolves into an uncertainty as between
                                                                        trespass
and a privileged connection with the woman which I don't
                                                                    understand.

We had come to stay for the Christmas holiday.
She was my grandmother.

A LAST LOOK BEFORE LEAVING

Suddenly she hadn't the heart to quarrel.
"He's faithless and won't change"
and with the thought was freed.
After he'd gone out, she packed
and put her suitcase by the door.
A last look before leaving.
The rug chosen together in Istanbul,
chess set lovingly given him.
"Three years and nothing."

She walked towards the traffic and hailed a taxi,
in her raised hand the black queen.

THE PAST

for Robert Beavis

We know so little.
A stone cries in the night.

Obstinate specks of clay
eclipse the glitter of brooch and ring.
A clasp no longer gathers unto itself.

We dig. We dig deeper,
touching the subtle fabric
of ancient ties.

A riot of unholy feeling prevented
the cracked vessel from ever being full –
or so we tentatively suggest.

The past hurts and our recourse
is to firm ground where
business employs and engrosses.

In snatches, letting go daily effort,
we feel both guilt and terror
for crimes which may also be ours.

Mistaken to picture our seed
running through lived lives,
a twist of exempted gold.

Were we taught
or do we know in our bones
the violent history of our kind?

What was suffered
is not transmitted. Dear
absence. Distant crucifixion.

Wild, beyond calculation.
Luminous passion. More life.

HER WAKING TRUTH

Out of the blue
her father's voice on the 'phone.
Despite the years of silence
his bluster was unmistakeable,
discharging at last
into what he wanted to say.
"Until we fix it
we'll be stuck at that moment."
As he spoke these words
she hung up.

An energetic walk,
clean air breathed deeply,
recovered calm as she pushed back.

Anger greeting the day
was her waking truth.
Bled into everything she did.
Could have said
"Betrayal cuts all the ties."
Waste of breath.
Father he'd never been.

Far cry.

LITHOGRAPH (black ink on white)

luminous image

    lake
          by stark means
                    conjured

          black
              describing white

gleam
      sifted
          through trees

         even still
              whiteness argues deep water

not two/not one
          black asserting

              white
                  asserting

ACTE SANS PAROLES

The interval
offers a brash music of trombones,
cymbal crashes and throbbing bass drum.
While they queue for ice-cream and candy floss,
families talk loudly through the din.
Unnoticed at the raised edge of the ring
a clown climbs onto a stool
where he perches
knees tucked up supporting his chin.
Against his painted face
he clutches the long stalk
of a pink carnation with both hands.

Now a spotlight picks him out.

As the audience begins to settle
a flustered girl brushes past him.
He straightens up, catches her eye
and with a bashful look
makes as if to give her the flower.
Their eyes meet.
With sudden courage he thrusts forward his lower hand
and is appalled when only the stalk is offered.
The bloom topples to the ground from the other hand.
His body droops
but he rallies and raises a finger.
She waits.

From inside his jacket he presents her with a rose.

R.C. Beavis

Originally from rural Suffolk, Robert first came to Bristol to study German. Vicissitude being what it is, he now holds a degree in Archaeology from the University of Bristol, and is particularly interested in the prehistory of Greece and the Balkan peninsula. Any resemblance to real persons, living or dead, is accidental.

The poems presented here are dedicated to the memory of Tony Howell.

LIMINA

Somewhere between water.
Not quite earth, not quite sky –
The year is still changing.

Settling mist over estuary,
Gravel ridge indistinct from convergences;
Grass, bank, strand shingled

Together, edging the world
Two rosehips survive
Red in the winter sun

POND

Still in the summer heat,
Not even the reflections move.

In fact, the sun,
Dozing across evening,

Waits for the day to cool.
Birdsong fades and falls asleep

In the overhanging trees.
Below, the water looks back at me.

A KITE ON ALDEBURGH BEACH

(for my father)

We assembled the kite on Aldeburgh beach,
A burst of colour on the pebbles.

Stick to stick, loop to loop, coming together like
Sinew and bone. The plastic frame placed

Firm, we held it to the wind –
Up, and up and circling with the gulls,

Lift and drag pulling friction
Burns through our fingers. My connecting

String snapped and I ran, headlong and
Tail-winded through the surf

ALBAICÍN

Stopping between faded pink grandeur and clear water,
I like to think she was Sephardic.
She showed me a two-headed bird in the
House where ibn Negrala's ghost levitates peaceably above a Moorish
Chair. Jews lived here once, waiting for the
Equinox to light their seven-stepped mikveh, but then
Torquemada got involved, expunging proud heraldries.

I stepped back onto streets paved with warmth and tired
Cats. The wind and narrow stole a
March on me: while astonished at a sprawl into
Mountains, I got lost not so much in geography as in time.

PIKE O'STICKLE

That's the word for it – a
Strange creature, round

As well as pointy. Death
Sharpened stickling rock, polished

It to a matt shine on the treacherous
Scree where life is as debitage.

I did not risk it.
I scrambled to the top

To take in Pavey Ark, where I was, and
Pike O' Blisco, where I have been.

NOCTURNE

The dark city swims, infinitudes
        splitting in the night waters,
          numberless streaks rising and sinking and

Rising – the harbourside floats – a whole
        city given life by the transports of
          its own brilliant reflection

The moon is a soft clarity unknown to day,
        suited to transepts and puddles;
          quicksilver bursts, the simple flash of

It, lending to mud and to rain and
        to the liquid city:

I, too, wish to bathe in crystal.

LITTLE VENICE

Evening terrace of barges
Lapped gently by dull
Water round invisible hulls.
Perched on the edges

Of the waterways' mergings,
They're more than just themselves,
Their own intimate lives
At the concrete verges

Of Little Venice, that
Odd nook halfway between
Warwick Avenue and Paddington.
It's almost too quiet,

Too tranquil for London –
A pleasantly overlooked corner
Nourished by our nostalgia
For an age gone

Long ago of boats,
Blue cast iron bridges
Rattling under Hackney carriages,
The scamper of brats

And of grubby urchins,
Their tiny bare feet
Pattering along streets
Straight out of Dickens.

EXCAVATION

The ground is hard, halfway to
Stone, packed safe round stone,
       its secrets kept,

Layered away from curious eyes.
Flow has no place down here
       in another time,

Meaning no validity. These
Things simply were, these black sherds
       where the earth

Cradled them. Exposed to rain and touches,
Trowelled up, a sacred confidence
       has been broken:

The long concealment of walls is violated
With tools, with hands, with novel thoughts,
       for unwanted measurement

Gillie Harries

Gillie Harries was born on the Suffolk coast and has lived in Bristol for the past 12 years. She has written poetry since childhood, and continues to write, publish and perform – from the Bristol Old Vic Studio to her local park and the Lookout Tower in Aldeburgh with Suffolk Poetry Society National Poetry Day 2015/2017, for example. Like Rilke she believes 'Poetry is the past, that breaks out in your heart'.

Gillie is a member of the collective of poets and musicians 'Echoes and Edges' and 'Bearing Witness'.

SHELTER

The azure cerulean numinous light,
Shimmer and glitter, warmth
As a gentled hand on a grieving heart.
The sea a cellophane skein
A bowl of gold.
Far, in the deeper blue
A jet arcs white counterpoint
Helps us on our way to reason.
Tamarisk, date palm, shiver in a breeze
Which drifts the water, refracts
To diamond light.
More distant still the heave and push
Of mountain solidity
Grounds our tremble
With all this beauty.
In the umbrella pine
A beneficent rooted tree
Of memory, its trunk striated
Supplicant branches,
Hold green so soft
You can taste its resinous bite
To the tongue.
New pale needles upright
As hopeful searching thought
Redemptive, forgiving
So verdant, its tenderness hurts.
Small birds nest there, helpless
Vulnerable as breath
In all this early perfect stillness.

GIFT

A small brief single syllable word
Velar plosive beginning, short vowel
Softening to close with fricative ease
And stop once more
Like a gate upon thought
Clicks to, a wooded lane behind us
In front a river tips itself over limestone
Smoothed like the path we may choose
But hesitate in dusk light
Pretending to halt to retie the lace
Of our well trodden boots,
Let companions walk on
We turn back
Lean on the mossed coolness
Of an old wall
Feel the stone indent our skin
Hear birdsong return
Breathe the evening
Unlatch ourself,
Weep a little even,
Then gather thought
Face west, the sun low
Softened by tears, so we may look
Stumble to a future
Not yet ours
But beckoning and yes
Bright even,
If we choose to make it ours
What else may we do?
In doing so
We honour those we love,
Loved us
Who even now
Would take our hand
Or place an arm about our shoulder
Lean us into their love
And on

In memory of David James Harries 17.09.1941 – 20.09.2011

EVERYTHING BEAUTIFUL HAS EDGES

Everything beautiful has edges
The safe boundary of a ribboned love
The wish for continuity
Not to live the unbidden life
Or stop by a field of grace
And regret you lost the key
To unlatch yourself at evening
Everything beautiful has edges
The Lady of Shalott
In her loveless tower
Unravelled by desire
Her prediction of demise
Her wish for an embroidered life
A symmetry of stitches
Of light and shadow
The selvedging of closure
Everything beautiful has edges
This page this book this room
Each a space of opportunity
The artist's hand, bounded by skin
Meeting surface of wood.
Even the sea, phantom with azure
Has somewhere an edge
Somewhere a return
Somewhere surely, an ending.

ETERNAL CREATION

I own this scarf, midnight silk
The label reads
'Hand Made by Tibetans in India'
Once displayed in a chic boutique
In Daylesford, Victoria
A mining place once
A spa town now
Where they peddle that
Nostalgia of colonialism
The Lucky Country.
This scarf is of a price of dollars
The Tibetans could not dream of counting
Let alone holding
In their gifted palms.
I chose it for my birthday.
This scarf is inky black
Almost weightless
Beautiful spirals
Of imperial peacock
Hand painted whorls
At either length
Of the rectangle -
Like prayer wheels.
At the delicate
Patiently stitched borders
Every half inch, precisely
A line of nine, small
Turquoise beads
Child-size work
Ends
In a dangle of smoky
Perspex discs
Like their eyes
At the horizon of a life -
Discs rattling like small birds
Settling at dusk

THE GRACE OF ACCURACY

The grace of accuracy
Is to have no requirement for accuracy
Setting out on a path
Linear with eastern light
Return to this shore of pebble crunch
And finding all along the need
Was to stop, breathe, be
In silence
And memory turns this way and that
In wan sunlit air
Like a crystal roped
On plumblined light
Now this shine
Now that opacity.
Discard the getting it right
Measuring all distance between
Now and then, here and now -
Just to stand by water
Allow its ebb to lap
Your small child's toes
High tide your heart.
Just to stand by water
Argent at heron lakes' margin
Shadowed with reed
Just to stand by water
Phosphorescent with loss
Just to stand by water
The castled ferry heaving to leave
Just to stand by water
Savour samphire's ozone bite
Just to stand by water
Pooled with estuarine light
Just to stand by water
With the certain knowledge
That this is the now of Life
Just to stand by water
This is the grace of accuracy

The title of the poem inspired by the line
"the grace of accuracy" Epilogue by Robert Lowell

Pete Weinstock

I live in Bristol and work in the world of drug treatment. My poems were once described as 'warm, humorous and moving' I hope they are. I write to explore the world and to manage strong or difficult feelings, but mainly for fun.

UNDER THE SKIN

If the universe had a shape, I fondly imagine it would be
the shape of an ever-expanding onion ... on its side.

Hey you onions, I know you:
beneath those tattered rags you wear,
your dried out papery skin,
combining shape and texture in the most pleasing way
different in size and colour
you test geometry to the limit.

You are friends with the elements
embraced and carried by the air,
loved by fire and water alike,
and you come from the earth.

You belong everywhere
revealing yourselves coyly from the soil
you: make soup, good and clear,
and hang in ropes from barns and kitchens.

You pickle yourselves in strong flavours from around the globe
lying in wait for the right time to gleam and shine.
you onions are something that can be known,
inside and out, in depth: deeper and deeper.

I observe how you welcome the knife
pleasing the cutter, dicing with life
you bathe in butter
basking: golden in the pan.

As I get beneath your skin,
the inner becomes the outer ... becomes the outer ...

more tears beneath each layer
like broken-hearted Russian dolls.

YOUNG WILLOWS

whipping the wind in the busy sky
saying: "go faster, go faster"
and the wind went faster
galloping across harvest fields
flinging stubbled straw high into the air
to catch and carry, sweeping and dusting
like a house-proud farmer's wife
after the balers have done their work
The willows bent and streaming like palms
surfing the monsoon winds
on hurricane beach
as the rain comes in from the sea
Cotton clouds mopped the light blue
wiping the rain
from the wind-screened sky
leaving it fresh and bright
Trees dance a wild dance
around the field's edge,
Outcrops proud and rocky
prance along the skyline
We stumble through gorse
tripping, slipping, scrambled
through rocks, scattered and brambled
across the sky-scraped hill

A BAG OF DRIED APRICOTS

a message to his lover
from Van Gogh
to say
'I'm not listening anymore'

proof that
summer
is happening
somewhere in the world

a reminder
oranges are not
the only fruit
strawberry is not the only jam

a recommendation
peaches on beaches
everywhere
use suntan lotion, always

A SINGULARITY

'Oh look! A ball of matter.' Mr Higgs gesticulated excitedly, 'I haven't seen one like that anywhere else.'

> 'No, it's the only one.'

'It's not very big is it?' Clearly disappointed, Mr Higgs spoke rather rudely.

> 'No, I should say about the size of an orange.'

'A what?' His tone: a mixture of confusion and surprise.

> 'An orange – it's a sort of fruit.'

'Wow! Did you see that? It exploded. That was a huge' his body now on full alert. 'Awesome!'

> 'That was a big bang, wasn't it. I'm pleased with that.'

'What were all those tiny things whizzing about?' a puzzled expression on Mr Higgs' face.

> 'Do you mean that mass of dust and matter flying outwards towards the far reaches of the universe?'

'No, just before that, there was a concentration of sub-visible particles about a thirteen-trillionth of a second after the explosion.' Mr Higgs' face was shining with intensity.

> 'No, I missed that.' said God, a bit miffed.

Mr Higgs continuing his train of thought said in a voice hesitant and uncertain 'I can't quite be sure but I think they were bosons.'

> 'OK, interesting. Well, I'd better get started, I've got a lot on this week.'

'OK God, good luck with your creation …' and was gone in an instant.

STRING THEORY

String: a marvellous thing,
terribly long, awfully thin,
it coils and weaves,
fastens and loosens
with adjustable angles,
tension and friction;
they invented a reel for hauling it in.

Without string Chinese kites would have flown away,
suspension bridges would not sway,
the Wright brothers:
would never get off the ground,
the wooden logic just wasn't sound;
even the wheel might not have gone far
probably not as far as the car.

Without string: knot technology would be a non-starter:
ropes, nets and cables dead in the water
and, sad though it would be for one kind of moth,
we wouldn't have invented most kinds of cloth;
clothes would be made from skin, not lamé.
There'd be no knitting, or sewing
or knotted macramé.

So essential is string to the human race
we use it in theories relating to space.
It keeps time on a tether
without string to hold it together
space would scatter and time wouldn't matter.
All things would fall apart
in a universe without string at its heart.

Charles Thompson

I like writing poems and I like writing plays. The theatricality of my writing of plays feeds my poems. I zestfully continue to explore this relationship.

I have a degree in English from Bristol University and a degree in Italian from the University of Kent. I have taught English in Italy, London, Dover, and Bath. I currently teach English to Somalian and Sudanese primary and secondary school pupils in Bristol.

I am developing an interest in the life of birds. I send my poems into the air like pink-footed geese to settle where they will.

I have had poems published in Poetry Monthly and Poetry Scotland.

ORPHEUS LAID-BACK IN THE SQUAT

Orpheus laid-back in the squat
Serenading distant stars;
Eurydice toiled at night
In drumming metro bars

Orpheus had to find her;
She could never make up her mind.
She'd gone back to a lover
He thought she'd left behind

And he imagined this as hell
And that she'd be on the rack
But she just disappeared
When she caught him looking back

And Jove locked up Prometheus
And said 'You can take a rest
From giving men what they say they need
Being tragic's what you do best!'

And by the Arch of Titus
Shelley scribbled notes
And wandered on to Pisa
And took to sailing boats.

I REMEMBER YOU, A HUNTING GIRL

I

'I remember you, a hunting girl.'

*'They said I was a witch
that – inside the church doors –
I sold my soul to the devil
for shining gold coins
and that the devil carried me off
on a black horse fitted with spikes.'*

'And you returned?
Tut tut, a tale like that!
But did I not meet you at the temple
clad in a fall of gold?
You told me you were a huntress.
I did not think you would kill Adonis
like that.'

*'But he was just that –
a vegetation god,'* you said

and took me to the fountain
where we washed and, afterwards,
ate fruit and slept.
and, the next day, hunted.

II

The reader pulled the aestle along
the lines of the Bible;
a rain of grace – it is said.

III

She spoke:

*'Dear friends all – I admire
your ebullience, your wit,
your greenness.'*

IV

And so, at last, I took
the short cut and found
a rustic hut
– beside a vinery clipped
to the warm brick of a wall –
The Temple of Vaccinia
they called it –
the pus of cow pox – did you know that?

V

all poets are healers
I thought

NOW THE MARRIED COUPLE DREAM

Now the married couple dream
Underneath the harvest moon
To roam beneath the sacred storm
All about field stubble corn
Cleaned with fire by farmers' work
And now the goldenrod shoots up
On woods and hedgerow cliff and hill
And thus and thus the bright asphodel
In peat and mire and flush and hill
Midsummer past
Demeter, her wreath of corn,
Her snake and pig sacred so
And how she finds Persephone
Within her fruitful fertile world
Of summer fig and apricot
And peaches, pears and poppyseed.
And how the pan pipes tremble far
In some wild-wood that no-one knows.

AND SO, DEAR FRIENDS, L'AVVOCATO

And so, dear friends, L'Avvocato
As plump he is as an avocado
Dauntless, jurado, bravado, el dorado
A roister-rooster 'Al Bar Marinaio'
Whose crow is gruff
Whose laugh is rough
A wit unforced
Rich, well-resourced,
Adapted, agile,
Oh no not fragile
A temper, balanced,
Just, on the razzle,
A man who handles local crooks
For crimes I would say mostly petty
And handles too his wife's spaghetti.
Sleep, eat, drink, law all uncomplicate
To live, laugh and intimidate
For an encore this grizzly bear
Intones with feeling 'My sweet-coloured pear
When I see you I feel brave'[1]
The simple lines the bright folk crave
'Piruç myò doç inculurit
quant yò chi viot, dut stoi ardit'[1]
Volcanic earthy a rumbling yarn
Round the rapt crowd the lyric Friulian.

[1.] The oldest-recorded Friulian poem

LA GIOIA

Gioia's laid-back boyfriend Marcello,
wore a soldier's shirt oh
dear, dear Gioia, how it hurt you
that this Marcello smoked so much pot and cursed
you said the whole day through

I remember once you said 'let's go
to my town – a Renaissance utopia
let's visit my folks in Palmanova';
off we bounced on the local train
sprinkle drizzle the sweet spring rain
'Here's Paolo, a studenty left-wing anarchy chap'
black scarf and black tumbled coat, no hat,
black hair that flooded wild about
and so Rita, Marco roundabout,
Rosmarino, a guy called Dante,
the geometric side streets to her folks' ristorante
where plump shortish dad, white apron, chef's hat,
stirred the pot which on a platform sat,
and while mum clucked about her girl,
a cowboy bloke all show and twirl
came in to have his spag and rosso
and roar approval 'delicioso'
E ancora, ancora bel rosso'

and, later, Gioia, a near fiance how he hurt you
by going off, after he'd met your grandma,
for a girl 'bruciante, bruciante'
allegro – I suppose – andante
and so, dear Gioia, when I met you last,
there – your flood forward on the river of your past
there – sky-blue dress – Etruscan – you
you – so lovely, quick and gentle too –
and there your carpenter chap, warm
upright, well-armed, a true Friulian,
and on a bench sucking thumbs
twins
with eyes like
the best
black plums

Lightning Source UK Ltd.
Milton Keynes UK
UKHW02f0013250518
323183UK00005B/61/P